Everyone wants to be like
Molly

For

Scott, Mum, Dad,

Kim, Carl and Jemma

Thank you

Chapter 1

Everyone wants to be like Molly

From day one at high school, the six girls had been inseparable. There had never been the squabbles or rivalry that split so many friendships. They were a unit. They were equal; none was more privileged in any way than the others.

Five years later, on their last day at school, they hugged and promised to stay best friends forever. However, the promise was soon broken as they spread further apart, each taking their own path in life.

The invitation that each woman held in her hand read;

You are invited to the 20th Anniversary for class 1992

How could twenty years have passed so quickly? Why hadn't they kept in touch?

Would they have changed? Would they still be friends?

Now after twenty years the friends were to be reunited.

Everyone envied Crystal. Although she hadn't done well at school, she had married well and owned outright a huge five bedroom house with a swimming pool and large garden. Her two children were at boarding school. Her husband worked long hours and was often away. She drove a brand new Mercedes sports car, wore designer clothes, and never had a chipped nail or a hair out of place. Her life was spent lunching, nights out and holidays, often alone. She would post her fabulous life on Facebook and Instagram so that everyone could see how amazing her life was.

In truth though, she was lonely, quite depressed and felt worthless. She had once been the trophy wife but then she had children and became 'the wife' and 'mother', putting up with her husband's affairs and trophy girlfriends.

How couldn't think of leaving. Without him she would have nothing. She wouldn't be able to afford her superficial life, and it was the only life she knew.

Deep down Crystal envied Molly. She had a husband and two children who were doing well at school, and a child-minder to care for them outside of school. Molly had gone to College and then University after leaving school.

Every morning she would leave home at 7.30 wearing her power suit, catch the train to the City. She and her husband had a large mortgage for their four bedroom house. They had turned the garage into a gym and had a hot tub in the garden. Even so, she would still go to the local health club twice a week on the way home from work. Molly seemed to have assistance with every aspect of life; her groceries were ordered online and delivered to her door. She had a cleaner three times a week, a gardener, window cleaner, and her Audi had a frequent valet.

Weekends were family time. They would go out as a family; often to the cinema, an art gallery, and museums or to see a show, walks in the countryside or a day trip to the seaside. Holidays were usually five star with plenty of activities for the children.

Molly seemed to be happy; although she had a busy life she

maintained her health by eating well, regular exercise, Yoga, Mindfulness and meditation. She knew how to apply herself and how to relax, making the most of herself and her life.

Carol also envied Molly. She had married at twenty-four, having the first of her two children two years later. Her husband owned his own business and worked hard to support them so that she could be a housewife and mother. They had a three bedroom house which always felt too small, cluttered and unorganized. As hard as she tried, Carol could not get on top of the housework. As the children grew and needed her less she lost her sense of worth. She would shop once a week but that was her only outing. She had few friends as most had returned to work. Her entire life felt trapped within the four walls of her home. She would often cry for no apparent reason. She began to fear going out and made up excuses on the rare occasion someone did suggest meeting up. Her children and husband treated her like a servant. She often thought about escaping. Her only way was suicide, but how could she do that to her family? She was stuck.

Jo however envied Carol, Molly and Crystal. Her marriage had ended in divorce ten years ago when her babies where two and four years old. She had met a nice man and remarried three years ago. He was a long distance lorry driver and often away. When he was at home, he was tired and would laze on the settee or go to bed to sleep the day away. He also had two children who stayed with them at the weekend and during the school holidays. Jo worked three part-time jobs as a cleaner. Her youngster son had ADHD and was Autistic. He would frequently need collecting early from school or need taking to appointments. She worked hard dashing from one job to the next, doing school runs, shopping, and heaving heavy bags on the bus as they couldn't afford to run two cars with such a large mortgage. She did everything for her own and extended family to make life run smoothly. She often ate junk food on the go, never exercised and once a month played Bingo with her friends. She was accepting of her life but knew that she was missing out. She didn't feel that she was worthy of any of the good things in life. She felt that life had dealt her a rough card. She felt put upon by her family and regularly moaned about how unfair it was that she had to do everything.

Even so, Sarah envied Jo as much as she envied all the others. She rented her two bedroom house with her daughter who had been born with Down syndrome. She had been in an abusive marriage and had left four years ago. She had started to study knowing that she needed to improve her prospects, but what was the point? Her life was filled with caring for her daughter. Sophie might grow older but she would always remain an eight year old child. They were both trapped by this condition. She worked part-time in a school as a Teaching Assistant but the pay was low and she wasn't popular because she continuously needed to be available for Sophie. Financially, she was ruined. She could barely cover the bills and would often go without food so that Sophie could have the things she needed; there was always something that needed to be paid for so that her daughter could have the best life possible.

She struggled through bouts of illness; usually unexplained and untreated. She could desperately benefit from help, but there was no one to help her. Both her parents had died in a car accident when she was twenty. Sophie didn't take well to strangers and after her abusive marriage, Sarah was not prepared to let another man get close to her. She didn't eat or sleep properly, she didn't exercise. She felt lonely, isolated and depressed.

However, she felt that she was in a better place than Sharon. She rented her two bedroom house. She didn't have a job so claimed benefit. She had three children and was expecting her fourth. She had low self-worth and had allowed men to treat her badly. She was incredibly lonely and depressed. She felt that she had more worth when she was in a relationship so a string of boyfriends came and went. She looked after her children the best she could but she couldn't really cope, especially with Billy, her youngest who had social anxiety. She had been pregnant with him when her Mum suddenly died of Cancer. She had never recovered from the trauma and felt that she was responsible for Billy's issues.

She wanted more from life. She wanted to have strength and courage. She wanted to be worth something. She wanted to be like Molly. Molly didn't have to live on junk food; Molly could afford to buy proper meat and vegetables. Molly wasn't over weight. She could afford the gym membership. Molly wasn't scraping by on benefits. She had a well-paid job. Molly didn't have to save the newspaper vouchers to go on holiday. She could afford a package holiday abroad. Molly didn't have to stress. Molly was lucky.

That's what they all thought as they talked about their lives and the turns they had taken during the last twenty years. Everyone thought that Molly was lucky. Everyone wanted to be like Molly.

Chapter 2

Molly's story

After leaving school with her friends, Molly had gone to college and then university where she achieved a degree in law. Durham was a long way from home but she soon settled and found love with Greg. Following their graduation they travelled the world for two years before returning to England, where they both found jobs and rented a flat. They married three years later and within a year they were expecting their first child.

Molly loved being a mum but part of her couldn't wait to get back to work. She had just finalized her return date when she discovered that she was pregnant again. She wasn't ready, and felt agitated throughout the pregnancy. Her mood was low and her body ached far more than with her first child. Labour was an exhausting eighteen hours and complicated. The baby wasn't receiving enough oxygen, so an emergency caesarean was needed to deliver the baby safely. He spent three weeks in the baby unit. They visited him every day and held his hand. Although she loved him dearly, she felt disconnected. They hadn't bonded. She felt she had failed him.

Finally the day came when they could take him home. Greg was amazing. He saw her struggle and took charge. He had taken one month paternity leave but that time was soon gone and she found herself home alone with her young daughter, who had mastered tantrums to perfection, and a constantly crying baby.

Over the next few months her depression became unbearable. Her mood was continuously low. She felt lethargic. She craved chocolate for regular boosts. She cried most of the day and when Greg returned from work she handed the children over to him and she went to bed. She hated herself for being like this. She felt she was a bad mother and wife. Greg bathed and fed the children then started on the housework. He dared not speak of what was going on for fear of Molly's reaction. They had started having tremendous rows over the slightest thing: things they would previously have laughed at.

Six months after the baby had been born, Molly was housebound; trapped indoors afraid to go out. She stopped taking her daughter to her playgroup and missed three appointments at the baby clinic. Finally, Greg arranged a home visit from the doctor who immediately diagnosed post-natal depression for which he prescribed antidepressants.

Within a few months she had started to feel like she could cope again. Her depression was masked rather than dealt with, but it was enough for her to start thinking about returning to work and the job she loved.

A year after Harry was born, she returned to work. The children were both happy in the nursery and Ellie excelled from being with other children. Molly began to feel that she was handling life well most of the time but found juggling work, the children and her home exhausting. She never had time for her to do what she wanted. It had been years since she had had a proper friend and she started to feel a guilty sense of dissatisfaction with life. She knew how lucky she was having Greg's support, two healthy children, a lovely home and a job she loved, but all the same she couldn't help dreaming of a different life; one where she was free. One where her partner was as romantic and as passionate as Greg used to be. One where she could be the Molly she once was rather than the woman that she had become.

Eighteen months after returning to work she received the devastating news that she was being made redundant. Times had changed and it was much harder to get another job. Nowhere seemed to need a qualified lawyer, and so she found herself back at home; jobless. Her sense of worth diminished, the children were happy in nursery and school. It wouldn't be fair to remove them. She felt she had nothing and now started to regret how she had coped after Harry was born. She had missed out on so much of his young life.

Greg reluctantly agreed to have another child. He was worried how he would cope if she went into depression again. Yet he knew how important this was to her self-worth. Within six months she was pregnant. She felt happier than she had in several years. She felt like she had finally got the hang of how she was meant to feel during pregnancy. She felt she had a real purpose in life again.

Fifteen weeks into the pregnancy she started feeling unwell. Then she started bleeding. Scared by what was happening, she called Greg and they rushed to the hospital. It was too late. She had had a miscarriage. Her world crumbled, her heart felt like it had literally broke.

The downward spiral that followed was quick. She became frustrated, angry, hated life and everyone in it. But none more than herself. She pushed Greg away and left him to care for their children. She didn't want or need any of them at that time. She needed food; comfort food. Chocolate, cake, biscuits – anything sweet, and TV. She didn't want to go out so there seemed no point in dressing. Greg could drop the children off and pick them up on his way to and from work. He could take them out at the weekend to do the grocery shop. He had always been a better cook than her and they preferred his meals, so she left him to do that too.

Greg was struggling; he couldn't cope with all of it. He didn't know what to do. She refused to take antidepressants again. He began to confide in a woman at work. She was single, attractive and understanding. She supported him in a way that he hadn't felt supported before. She understood him like Molly used to. It wasn't long before they had started their affair that lasted six months.

Of course, Molly knew. He didn't need to say. She noticed the increased text messages he received and the smile that he tried to contain as he read them; The later time he picked the children up and came home; His improved mood; The new 'boys' from work he had agreed to befriend and see once a week. And why wouldn't he have an affair? She had made life difficult for him. She still loved him. She didn't want their marriage to end or their family to break up. She had to do something before she lost everything.

Chapter 3

Initial report for Molly Smith by Tracey Chivers

When Molly first came to me she had tried a whole range of therapies; Cognitive Behavioural Therapy, Coaching, Counselling, Meditation, Yoga and Mindfulness to name a few. Whilst some of these had made an impact and brought her some benefit, Molly said she still needed something different; something she could hold onto to change who she was forever; Something long-term, 'not something that will last a few weeks and then wear off again'.

Below are the initial questions I asked Molly and her responses:

Molly, how do you feel you should change?

I think I should be more motherly, more focused on my family, more caring and considerate... to be in a better mood…to get a job…sort out my marriage. I've just got to change to be better at all of it.

Why do you feel you need to change?

Because I make other people not like me, especially Greg. The children can't like me much and I don't have much contact with my friends now…I don't think they liked the way I was going… It hurts and upsets me. If I change they might like me again.

Do you like yourself Molly?

No

Have you ever liked yourself?

Yes

Molly, like so many women (and men), has lost who she is; the sense of herself. There is no recollection of it happening, as usually it is at a very early age but we only realize later in life when issues arise and force us to value ourselves.

We all come to Earth as spiritual beings to have a human experience. We don't know how to be human. We learn; early in life. Within the first few years we have learnt to talk, walk, eat, dress etc. We have learnt the functional skills of Earth but then we start to learn emotions, feelings and responses. For example, we learn anger, jealousy, emotional pain and resentment of those who hurt us.

But, what if we never experience those things? What if we lived our lives without the suffering? Would we be happy? Would we be living akin to our spiritual nature?

When I put this to Molly she seemed intrigued. "I know I was a happy child" she said "and I remember when I first started to doubt or dislike myself". The children in her primary school had laughed at her for having a limp. "I started to dislike my legs because they weren't normal but I still thought that I was okay as a person…it was just my legs".

That was the point at which Molly changed from a spiritual being into a human being. She allowed the outside world to dictate and create a discord in her own inner world. From that point on she had responded to every situation in her life as a human being; not as a spiritual being having a human experience, so by the time she was an adult with real issues, difficult issues to deal with, she found that the outside world was beating her up and she was allowing it to happen; agreeing with what she thought the outside world was telling her.

———

Molly's transformation took place when she let go of her belief that the outside world must dictate her inside world. She quickly learned the three principles to 'Inner tranquillity'. Her coaching lasted eighteen months. In which time she reconnected with her true self. She continued to be a great mum and started her dream job.

I say she continued to be a great mum because she always had been. It was her own thoughts that had suggested

that she was a bad mum. The reality
was not what she thought. The reality
was that Molly was doing the best she
could at the time with what she had
given herself in life.

Her psychological nature had been
humanized and was out of kilter with her
spiritual nature. Once they were
harmonized, Molly was more content;
she found herself again and moved on
to be the successful woman it was
always intended she would be.

Inner Tranquillity

Inner Tranquillity works on the principle that we are spiritual beings having human experiences. We wear the uniform of the body to exist on Earth. When we allow ourselves to become humanized we no longer feel our spiritual self. Life goes wrong when we are disconnected and don't take notice of our intuition.

This theory is not based on any religious beliefs. It is based on three facts:

1. We are a very small part of a much larger universe that functions independently from us. I (you, we) are part of a larger whole and I (you, we) are not in charge of how things unfold. The larger whole can be referred to as the Universe, God, Spirit etc. The label is not important.

Therefore you should call it whatever feels right for you.

2. Our awareness of the universe; of its endless love and beauty. Its ability to provide everything that is needed for the existence of all living things.
   Our awareness is internal as well as external. We recognize how our emotions and feelings determine our mood and how we view life. How you view your world is a result of your awareness. The more aware you are the better view you have. The better you feel about the view, the better your mood will be.

3. Thoughts give us guidance. The slightest shift in our thoughts changes our emotions, feelings and mood. Realizing that your response to life is the result of your thoughts allows you to

change your thoughts and your life.

Inner Tranquillity coaching is like pressing the re-set button. It allows you to realign with your factory settings so that you can live the life you were intended to live.

Thank you for reading this book. My hope is that every woman who reads it and identifies with at least one of the characters will take inspiration from Molly.   Life is for living, not for suffering, existing or enduring. You were born to live. Be yourself and true to yourself.

Press the re-set button.

With love

Tracey

P.S. If you would like to get in-touch I would love to hear from you.

Tracey@annaley.net

Live as

A spiritual being having a
human experience

Rather than

A human being having a
spiritual experience.

Printed in Great Britain
by Amazon